52-WEEK

DEVOTIONAL

FOR

TEEN GIRLS

Published by Midsummer Bloom Books

First Edition: September 2025
Printed in the United States of America

Contents

Introduction

Hey there, beautiful soul!

I'm so glad you picked up this book. Whether someone gave it to you, you found it on your own, or you're just curious about what God has to say—welcome. This devotional was written just for you, a teen girl navigating one of the most exciting, confusing, and transformative seasons of life.

Let's be real—being a teen girl today isn't easy. School pressure, friend drama, family expectations, social media, and figuring out who you are can feel overwhelming. Some days you're flying high, and other days you wonder if anyone really understands what you're going through.

Here's the truth: God sees you. He knows every struggle, every tear, every joy, and every dream in your heart. He's not distant or disconnected—He cares deeply about every part of your life.

This devotional is your weekly companion for a year, diving into themes like friendships, self-worth, anxiety, purpose, relationships, and faith. Together, we'll explore what God's Word says about these topics and discover how His truth can transform your life.

You don't need to be a Bible expert—just come with an open heart. Take your time, journal your thoughts, and talk to God about what you're learning. This journey isn't about perfection but about growing closer to the One who loves you perfectly.

Ready to see how much God adores you and what He has planned for your life? Let's dive in!

Week 1: You Are Loved More Than You Know

God's Truth

"See what kind of love the Father has given to us, that we should be called children of God; and so we are. The reason why the world does not know us is that it did not know him."–1 John 3:1 (ESV)

Devotional Thought

Have you ever stood under a starry sky and felt incredibly small? Now imagine the God who created billions of galaxies knows your name, counts your tears, and celebrates your victories. That's not just a nice thought – it's the absolute truth about your life.

You are not loved because of your grades, your appearance, or how many likes you get on social media. You're loved simply because you exist, because God chose to create you and call you His daughter. This love isn't earned through perfect behavior or lost through mistakes. It's constant, unchanging, and deeper than any human love you'll ever experience.

Think about the most loved you've ever felt – maybe when your mom hugged you after a hard day, or when your best friend knew exactly what to say. God's love is infinitely greater than that. He loved you before you were born, loves you right now as you read this, and will love you through every single moment of your future.

When 1 John calls us "children of God," it's not just a title – it's an identity that changes everything. You belong to the King of the universe. You have a Father who will never leave you, never give up on you, and never love you any less than He does right now.

A Prayer for You

Dear God, help me grasp how deeply You love me. When I feel unworthy, remind me that I'm Your precious daughter. When loneliness creeps in, wrap me in Your presence. Let Your love be the foundation of my identity today and always. Amen.

Your Challenge

This week, write "I am loved by God" on three sticky notes and place them where you'll see them daily – your mirror, phone case, or school locker. Each time you see one, pause for five seconds and let that truth sink into your heart. Notice how this simple reminder changes your perspective throughout the day.

Take a Moment

Close your eyes and place your hand over your heart. Feel it beating. That rhythm is proof that God is sustaining your life right this second. Take five deep breaths, and with each one, imagine God's love filling you up like warm sunshine. Let yourself simply receive His love without trying to earn it or understand it completely.

Week 2: When Anxiety Takes Over

God's Truth

"Cast all your anxiety on him because he cares for you."–1 Peter 5:7 (ESV)

Devotional Thought

That test tomorrow. The group project where no one's doing their part. The conversation you need to have with your friend. The college applications looming ahead. Your mind races at 2 AM, creating worst-case scenarios that feel so real you can barely breathe. Sound familiar?

Anxiety tells you that you're alone in carrying these burdens, that everything depends on you getting it all right. But God offers a radically different approach: cast your anxieties on Him. The word "cast" here literally means to throw or hurl. God isn't asking you to gently hand over your worries – He's inviting you to throw them at Him with all your might.

Why? Because He cares for you. Not just about you, but for you. Like a parent who stays up all night with a sick child, God is personally invested in your wellbeing. Your anxiety doesn't make you weak or less spiritual. Even Jesus felt overwhelmed in the garden of Gethsemane. The difference is knowing you don't have to carry it alone.

When anxiety floods your mind, remember: the God who holds the universe together can certainly handle your tomorrow. He's not overwhelmed by your problems or annoyed by your fears. He's ready and waiting to carry what's too heavy for you.

A Prayer for You

Lord, my anxiety feels so heavy right now. I'm throwing all my worries at You – every fear, every "what if," every over-whelming thought. Replace my anxiety with Your peace. Help me trust that You're working even when I can't see it. Hold me close today. Amen.

Your Challenge

Create an "anxiety playlist" with five worship songs that calm your spirit. When anxious thoughts spiral, put in your head-phones and let truth wash over your mind. Share this playlist with a friend who might need it too. Music has a powerful way of redirecting our thoughts toward God's faithfulness.

Take a Moment

Find a comfortable position and try the 5-4-3-2-1 grounding technique with a spiritual twist. Name 5 things you can see that remind you of God's creation, 4 things you can touch while thanking God for them, 3 things you can hear while listening for His presence, 2 things you can smell, and 1 thing you can taste. This brings you back to the present moment where God meets you.

Week 3: Your Value Isn't Defined by Social Media

God's Truth

"For we are his workmanship, created in Christ Jesus for good works, which God prepared beforehand, that we should walk in them."-
Ephesians 2:10 (ESV)

Devotional Thought

You post a photo you love, then refresh constantly, watching the likes slowly climb. Or worse, they don't. Suddenly that confidence you felt vanishes, replaced by questions: Am I pretty enough? Interesting enough? Worth following? Social media has become a 24/7 report card on your value, and it's exhausting.

Here's what Instagram will never tell you: you are God's workmanship. The Greek word used here is "poiema," where we get the word "poem." You are God's poetry, His masterpiece, His work of art. Before filters existed, before anyone double-tapped anything, God was crafting you with intentional, artistic precision.

Your value was set before you posted your first selfie. It doesn't fluctuate with your follower count or story views. God didn't create you to perform for likes; He created you for good works He's already prepared. While social media shouts about your appearance and popularity, God whispers about your purpose and potential.

Those perfectly curated feeds you scroll through? They're highlight reels, not real life. But you? You're real, valuable, and loved beyond any algorithm's ability to calculate. Your worth isn't measured in hearts and comments but in the price God paid for you – His own Son.

A Prayer for You

God, free me from the trap of seeking validation through screens. Help me see myself through Your eyes, not through filters or follower counts. When I'm tempted to measure my worth by likes, remind me I'm already loved beyond measure by You. Amen.

Your Challenge

Take a 24-hour social media break this week. During the times you'd usually scroll, do something that feeds your soul – read, create art, call a friend, or spend time in nature. Notice how your mood and self-perception change when you're not constantly comparing yourself to others online.

Take a Moment

Stand in front of a mirror and instead of critiquing what you see, speak three specific things God might say about you. Not about your appearance, but about your heart, your gifts, your potential. Let God's truth about who you are drown out social media's lies about who you should be.

Week 4: Navigating Friendship Challenges

God's Truth

"A friend loves at all times, and a brother is born for adversity."–Proverbs 17:17 (ESV)

Devotional Thought

She said she'd keep your secret, but now everyone knows. Your friend group is splitting, and you're caught in the middle. The girl you thought was your best friend suddenly seems distant. Friendship in high school can feel like navigating a minefield where one wrong step changes everything.

Real friendship isn't just about having fun together or sharing inside jokes – it's about loving through the messy, complicated times. When Proverbs says a friend loves "at all times," it means during arguments, misunderstandings, and even betrayals. This doesn't mean staying in toxic friendships, but it does mean approaching friendship challenges with grace.

Maybe you're the one who messed up, said something hurtful, or broke trust. True friendship includes humility to apologize and courage to make things right. Or perhaps you're the one hurt, wondering if the friendship can survive. God calls you to forgiveness, even when it's hard.

Jesus modeled perfect friendship – He was betrayed, denied, and abandoned by His closest friends, yet He loved them still. He shows us that real friendship sometimes means having difficult conversations, setting boundaries, and choosing love even when feelings are hurt. Not every friendship will last forever, but every friendship can teach you about love, forgiveness, and growth.

A Prayer for You

Lord, friendship feels so complicated right now. Give me wisdom to know when to speak up and when to stay quiet, when to hold on and when to let go. Help me be the friend You've called me to be. Amen.

Your Challenge

Reach out to a friend you've been having tension with or someone you've been meaning to reconnect with. Send a simple, honest message without expecting anything in return. Sometimes healing starts with one brave person taking the first step toward restoration.

Take a Moment

Think of three friends who have impacted your life positively. Spend a minute praying specifically for each one, asking God to bless them today. Don't tell them you're praying – just let it be a secret gift between you and God. Notice how praying for others shifts your heart toward love.

Week 5: When You Feel Like You Don't Belong

God's Truth

"But you are a chosen race, a royal priesthood, a holy nation, a people for his own possession, that you may proclaim the excellencies of him who called you out of darkness into his marvelous light."–1 Peter 2:9 (ESV)

Devotional Thought

You walk into the cafeteria and every table seems full of inside jokes you're not part of. You sit in class feeling invisible while everyone else seems to belong somewhere. That ache of not fitting in can feel overwhelming, like you're on the outside of life looking in.

But here's what changes everything: before you were born, God chose you. Not as a last pick or reluctant addition, but as His treasured possession. You belong to the King of kings, which makes you royalty. When earthly groups reject you, remember you're already part of the most important family in existence.

Feeling like you don't belong isn't always bad – sometimes it's because God set you apart for something special. You weren't created to blend in perfectly with everyone else. You were made to stand out, to bring something unique that only you can offer. Your differences aren't flaws; they're features God intentionally designed.

That loneliness you feel? Jesus felt it too. He was misunderstood, rejected, and alone, even among crowds. He understands that hollow feeling in your chest. But He also promises you're never truly alone. You belong to Him, and nothing can change that status.

A Prayer for You

God, when I feel like I don't fit anywhere, remind me I belong to You. Help me find my identity in being Your daughter, not in being accepted by others. Show me where You want me to shine Your light today. Amen.

Your Challenge

This week, look for someone else who seems to be on the outside and intentionally include them. Invite them to sit with you, start a conversation, or simply smile and say hello. Sometimes the best way to heal our own loneliness is to ease someone else's.

Take a Moment

Create a mental "belonging inventory." Instead of listing where you don't fit, list where you do belong: God's family, your home, that one class where you excel, the activity you love. Focus on expanding these spaces of belonging rather than forcing yourself into spaces that weren't meant for you.

Week 6: True Beauty Comes From Within

God's Truth

"Do not let your adorning be external—the braiding of hair and the putting on of gold jewelry, or the clothing you wear—but let your adorning be the hidden person of the heart with the imperishable beauty of a gentle and quiet spirit, which in God's sight is very precious."–1 Peter 3:3-4 (ESV)

Devotional Thought

You spend an hour getting ready, and one glance in the harsh school bathroom lighting destroys your confidence. Everyone else seems to have perfect skin, perfect hair, perfect everything. The pressure to look flawless is crushing, and no amount of makeup or outfit changes seems to be enough.

God isn't against you caring about your appearance – He created beauty and appreciates it. But He knows something the world doesn't: external beauty is temporary, while inner beauty grows more radiant with time. That gentle and quiet spirit Peter mentions isn't about being shy or silent; it's about having a peaceful confidence that comes from knowing whose you are.

Think about the most beautiful person you know – not Instagram beautiful, but truly beautiful. Chances are, it's someone whose kindness lights up their face, whose joy is contagious, whose love makes everyone feel valued. That's the imperishable beauty God is cultivating in you.

Your body is changing, skin breaks out, bad hair days happen – that's all normal and temporary. But every time you choose kindness, every moment you extend grace, every day you trust God, you're developing a beauty that will never fade. This beauty can't be bought, filtered, or faked. It's precious in God's sight and magnetic to others.

A Prayer for You

Lord, help me see beauty the way You do. When I obsess over my appearance, redirect my energy toward developing inner beauty. Let my confidence come from being Your beloved daughter, not from meeting impossible beauty standards. Make me truly beautiful from the inside out. Amen.

Your Challenge

For one week, limit mirror time to basic hygiene needs. Instead of multiple appearance checks throughout the day, use those moments to check your heart. Ask yourself: How can I show kindness? How can I reflect God's love? Notice how this shift changes both your confidence and your impact on others.

Take a Moment

Think of a specific quality you want to develop in your inner beauty – perhaps patience, joy, or compassion. Visualize yourself displaying this quality in tomorrow's situations. See yourself responding with patience when frustrated, choosing joy despite circumstances, or showing compassion to someone difficult. This mental practice prepares your heart for real-life beauty moments.

Week 7: Handling Crushes and Relationships

God's Truth

"Above all else, guard your heart, for everything you do flows from it."-Proverbs 4:23 (ESV)

Devotional Thought

Your heart races when he walks by. You analyze every text for hidden meanings. You daydream about possibilities and wonder if he notices you exist. Crushes can make you feel like you're floating and drowning at the same time. These feelings are normal, exciting, and sometimes overwhelming.

God isn't surprised by your feelings – He designed you with the capacity to love and be loved. But He also knows how vulnerable your heart is right now. Guarding your heart doesn't mean building walls so high that no one can enter. It means being intentional about who you allow to influence your emotions, decisions, and self-worth.

That guy you like? He might be wonderful, but he's not your savior. No human relationship can fill the God-shaped space in your heart. When you try to make someone else your everything, you'll always end up disappointed because only God can be everything you need.

Healthy relationships – whether they're beginning crushes or something more – start with knowing your worth in Christ. When you're secure in God's love, you won't desperately chase after someone's attention or compromise your values for acceptance. You'll be able to recognize the difference between someone who honors you and someone who just flatters you.

A Prayer for You

God, these feelings are so intense and confusing sometimes. Help me guard my heart while still being open to healthy relationships. Show me the difference between Your plan and my fantasies. Keep me grounded in Your love above all else. Amen.

Your Challenge

Write down three non-negotiable values for any relationship (like respect, shared faith, or kindness). When crushes develop, check these values before letting your emotions run wild. This isn't about having a checklist for perfection, but about recognizing what truly matters beyond butterflies and excitement.

Take a Moment

Imagine your future self at 25, looking back at your teenage years. What advice would she give you about crushes and relationships? What would she say matters most? Let this perspective guide your choices now. Remember, every decision you make today is shaping the woman you're becoming.

Week 8: When Family Feels Hard

God's Truth

"Children, obey your parents in the Lord, for this is right. 'Honor your father and mother' (this is the first commandment with a promise), 'that it may go well with you and that you may live long in the land.'"–Ephesians 6:1-3 (ESV)

Devotional Thought

Your mom doesn't understand you. Your dad's expectations feel impossible. Your siblings drive you crazy. Maybe your family is going through divorce, financial stress, or other heavy situations. Some days, home feels like the hardest place to be, and you wonder why God placed you in this particular family.

Honoring your parents doesn't mean they're always right or that your feelings don't matter. It means choosing respect even when you disagree, showing love even when you're frustrated. This is especially hard when your parents are imperfect, make mistakes, or don't understand your world. But God's command comes with a promise – that it will go well with you.

Sometimes honoring looks like having honest, respectful conversations about how you feel. Sometimes it means accepting that your parents are doing their best with their own struggles. It might mean forgiving them daily for not being the parents you wish you had, while appreciating who they are.

Your family might not look like the perfect families on social media, but God placed you exactly where you are for a reason.

He's using even the difficult dynamics to shape you, teach you, and prepare you for your future. Every challenge at home is an opportunity to practice grace, patience, and unconditional love.

A Prayer for You

Lord, family is really hard right now. Give me patience when I want to explode and wisdom to honor my parents even when I don't understand them. Help me see my family through Your eyes and love them like You do. Bring healing where we need it. Amen.

Your Challenge

This week, do one unexpected act of kindness for a family member you've been struggling with. Make their favorite snack, clean up without being asked, or write an encouraging note. Don't expect anything in return – just let love be your motivation and see how it shifts the atmosphere.

Take a Moment

Picture Jesus sitting at your dinner table tonight, observing your family dynamics. How would His presence change the conversation? The attitudes? The responses? Carry this image with you and let it influence how you interact with your family today. Remember, Jesus understands complicated families – His own family thought He was crazy at one point!

Week 9: Discovering Your Unique Purpose

God's Truth

"The heart of man plans his way, but the Lord establishes his steps." — Proverbs 16:9 (ESV)

Devotional Thought

Everyone seems to know what they want to do with their lives except you. College majors, career paths, life goals – the pressure to have it all figured out feels suffocating. You wonder if you're falling behind, if you're missing some obvious sign about your purpose, if maybe you don't have anything special to offer.

Here's the truth that changes everything: God prepared good works specifically for you before you were even born. Not for the girl sitting next to you in chemistry, not for your incredibly talented friend, but for you. Your purpose isn't something you have to manufacture or discover through career tests. It's already been written into your story by the Author himself.

Your purpose right now might not be some grand, world-changing mission. It might be encouraging that lonely freshman, using your artistic gifts to bring beauty into spaces, or simply being a light in your family. God rarely reveals the entire blueprint at once. Instead, He shows you the next step, then the next, building your purpose one obedient moment at a time.

Stop comparing your chapter three to someone else's chapter twenty. Your gifts, experiences, and even your struggles are all threads God is weaving into a beautiful purpose. Trust the process, even when you can't see the pattern yet.

A Prayer for You

God, I feel so much pressure to figure out my entire future right now. Help me trust that You've already prepared my purpose. Show me what good works You have for me today, and give me courage to walk in them. Amen.

Your Challenge

This week, pay attention to what makes you come alive – what problems upset you, what activities make you lose track of time, what compliments you consistently receive. Write these observations down. Often, our purpose is hidden in plain sight, in the things that feel so natural we overlook them.

Take a Moment

Imagine God as a master artist, painting your life's purpose. Some sections are detailed and clear, others are still rough sketches. Instead of demanding to see the finished painting, appreciate the strokes He's adding today. Trust that the Artist knows what He's doing, even when the painting looks incomplete to you.

Week 10: Overcoming School Stress

God's Truth

"Commit your work to the Lord, and your plans will be established."-Proverbs 16:3 (ESV)

Devotional Thought

Three tests this week. A project due tomorrow you haven't started. Your GPA determining your entire future – or at least it feels that way. The pressure to excel, to keep up, to somehow balance academics with everything else feels impossible. You're drowning in assignments while trying to stay afloat emotionally, and nobody seems to understand how overwhelmed you really are.

God cares about your education, but not for the reasons you might think. He's not checking your report card or disappointed when you get a B instead of an A. He cares because He knows the character, discipline, and perseverance you're developing through these challenges will serve you long after you've forgotten the quadratic formula.

Committing your work to the Lord doesn't mean praying for straight A's and expecting them to magically appear. It means doing your best with the time and energy you have, then trusting God with the results. It means remembering that your worth isn't determined by your class rank. It means finding peace even in the middle of academic chaos.

When stress threatens to overwhelm you, remember: the God who gave Solomon wisdom, who helped Daniel excel in

Babylonian schools, who gave Jesus understanding beyond His years – this same God is with you in every classroom, every test, every assignment.

A Prayer for You

Lord, school feels so overwhelming right now. Help me manage my time wisely and retain what I'm learning. When anxiety about grades consumes me, remind me that You're more concerned with who I'm becoming than what I'm achieving. Give me Your peace. Amen.

Your Challenge

Create a "stress-less study routine" this week: Set a timer for 25-minute focused study sessions with 5-minute breaks. During breaks, don't check social media – instead, stretch, pray, or step outside. Notice how working with intentional breaks actually helps you accomplish more while feeling less overwhelmed.

Take a Moment

Before your next big test or assignment, pause and take three deep breaths. With each exhale, release the pressure to be perfect. With each inhale, receive God's wisdom and peace. Remember that in ten years, you won't remember this specific test, but you'll remember how you learned to handle pressure with grace.

Week 11: Stop Comparing, Start Thriving

God's Truth

"But he said to me, 'My grace is sufficient for you, for my power is made perfect in weakness.' Therefore I will boast all the more gladly of my weaknesses, so that the power of Christ may rest upon me."–2 Corinthians 12:9 (ESV)

Devotional Thought

She's prettier, smarter, more talented. Her life looks perfect while yours feels like a mess. You scroll through highlight reels, sit in classrooms, walk through hallways constantly measuring yourself against everyone else. Comparison has become your default mode, and you always seem to come up short. This exhausting race has no finish line because there's always someone seemingly doing better.

God's economy works differently than the world's ranking system. Where you see weakness, He sees opportunity for His strength. Where you see lack, He sees space for His abundance. Your weaknesses aren't disqualifications; they're invitations for God's power to shine through you in ways it never could through someone who seems to have it all together.

That girl you're comparing yourself to? She's fighting battles you know nothing about. She's comparing herself to someone else, feeling inadequate in ways that would surprise you. This comparison game has no winners, only exhausted players who never feel good enough.

God isn't asking you to be the best at everything. He's asking you to be yourself – the real, authentic, imperfect you that He purposefully created. When you embrace your unique story, strengths, and even struggles, you stop competing and start completing the specific role only you can fill.

A Prayer for You

God, I'm so tired of comparing myself to everyone else. Help me see that You've given me exactly what I need for my unique journey. Transform my weaknesses into displays of Your strength. Free me to thrive as myself. Amen.

Your Challenge

For one week, when you catch yourself comparing, immediately name one thing you're grateful for about your own life or abilities. Train your brain to shift from comparison to gratitude. Keep a running list and watch how your perspective changes when you focus on your blessings rather than others' perceived advantages.

Take a Moment

Picture yourself and the person you compare yourself to most standing before God. See Him delighting in both of you equally, not comparing or ranking, just loving. He's not disappointed that you're not her. He's thrilled that you're you. Let this image settle deep in your heart.

Week 12: Trusting God's Perfect Timing

God's Truth

"For everything there is a season, and a time for every matter under heaven."–Ecclesiastes 3:1 (ESV)

Devotional Thought

Everyone else seems to be experiencing things before you – first relationships, driver's licenses, freedom, opportunities. You feel stuck in slow motion while life races past you. You pray and wait, wait and pray, wondering if God forgot about your requests or if maybe He's punishing you with delays. The waiting feels unbearable.

But God's timing isn't slow – it's perfect. Every "not yet" is actually God's protection, preparation, or redirection. That relationship you desperately want? God might be preparing you to handle it with wisdom. That opportunity that passed you by? God might be saving you from something that looked good but would've derailed His better plan.

Think about a flower blooming. If you force it open before its time, you destroy it. But when it opens naturally, in its season, the beauty is breathtaking. You're not behind schedule; you're right on time for your unique journey. God is preparing you, not punishing you. He's developing strength, character, and faith that rushing would bypass.

Your friends might be experiencing certain milestones first, but that doesn't make your story less valuable. God is writing a story specifically for you, with perfect timing for each chapter. Trust the Author. He knows exactly when to turn the page.

A Prayer for You

Lord, waiting is so hard. When I feel left behind, remind me You're not slow but perfectly timing every detail of my life. Help me trust Your schedule over my demands. Give me patience to wait and wisdom to grow during this season. Amen.

Your Challenge

Create a "While I Wait" list of things you can do during this season of waiting – develop skills, deepen friendships, grow spiritually, serve others. Instead of just waiting for something to happen, actively engage in preparing yourself for when it does. Make waiting productive rather than passive.

Take a Moment

Think of something you desperately wanted in the past but didn't get, and now you're grateful it didn't happen. Remember how painful that waiting was, but how clear God's protection became later. Apply this perspective to your current waiting. Trust that future you will understand what present you cannot see.

Week 13: The Fear of Missing Out (FOMO)

God's Truth

"The Lord is my shepherd; I shall not want. He makes me lie down in green pastures. He leads me beside still waters."–Psalm 23:1-2 (ESV)

Devotional Thought

Your phone buzzes with notifications from the party you weren't invited to. Stories show everyone having the time of their lives while you're home on a Friday night. The fear of missing out gnaws at you, making you feel invisible, forgotten, unwanted. You wonder what's wrong with you and why you're always on the outside of the fun.

David declared "I shall not want" because he trusted his Shepherd to lead him exactly where he needed to be. Sometimes God leads you beside still waters when everyone else seems to be at the party by the loud waters. This isn't punishment or rejection – it's purposeful placement. God knows what you need more than you do.

That event you're missing might look amazing on social media, but God might be protecting you from compromising situations, toxic relationships, or distractions from His better plan. Or He might simply be teaching you that your worth isn't determined by your social calendar. Not every opportunity is your opportunity. Not every experience is meant for your story.

FOMO assumes that excitement and inclusion equal fulfillment, but God offers something better – contentment in His presence. When you trust that God is placing you exactly where you need to be, FOMO loses its power. You're not missing out; you're being set apart for something better.

A Prayer for You

God, FOMO makes me feel so left out and unimportant. Help me trust that You're leading me to exactly where I need to be. Replace my fear of missing out with joy in what You're doing in my life right now. Amen.

Your Challenge

Next time FOMO strikes, instead of scrolling through what you're missing, create your own meaningful moment. Call a grandparent, write in a journal, learn something new, or do something kind for someone else. Document this for yourself (not social media) and discover that joy doesn't require an invitation.

Take a Moment

Close your eyes and imagine Jesus sitting with you right now, choosing your company over any party or event. He's not missing out by being with you – you're His first choice. Feel the peace of being fully chosen and wanted by the Creator of the universe. Let His presence be enough.

Week 14: When You Mess Up Big

God's Truth

"If we confess our sins, he is faithful and just to forgive us our sins and to cleanse us from all unrighteousness."–1 John 1:9 (ESV)

Devotional Thought

You did the thing you swore you'd never do. Said words you can't take back. Made a choice that disappointed everyone, including yourself. Now shame sits heavy on your chest, replaying your mistake on repeat. You wonder if God is as disappointed as you are, if this mess-up finally pushed His love too far.

Here's what the enemy doesn't want you to know: your biggest mistake is no match for God's forgiveness. The moment you confess, God forgives. Not after you've beaten yourself up enough, not after you've proven you're really sorry, but immediately. His faithfulness to forgive doesn't depend on the size of your sin but on the size of His love.

That cleansing John talks about? It's complete. God doesn't forgive you but keep a file of your failures for later. He wipes the slate completely clean, seeing you as pure as if the mistake never happened. This isn't because sin doesn't matter, but because Jesus already paid the price for every single mess-up, including this one.

Your mistake doesn't define you – God's mercy does. Yes, there might be earthly consequences to navigate, relationships to repair, trust to rebuild. But with God? You're already forgiven, already loved, already given a fresh start. That's the scandal of grace.

A Prayer for You

God, I messed up so badly and I can't seem to forgive myself. Help me receive Your complete forgiveness. Remove this crushing shame and replace it with Your peace. Thank You for loving me even at my worst. Give me courage to make things right where I can. Amen.

Your Challenge

Today, confess your mistake to God out loud, then say "I receive Your forgiveness" three times. Stand up, take a deep breath, and physically walk forward three steps, symbolizing moving forward from this moment. Your mistake is part of your story, but it's not the end of your story.

Take a Moment

Place your hand over your heart and feel it beating. That heartbeat is proof that God hasn't given up on you. He's still sustaining your life, still has plans for you, still sees beauty in your future. Take five deep breaths, and with each exhale, release a piece of shame. With each inhale, receive God's fresh mercy.

Week 15: Finding Calm in the Chaos

God's Truth

"Peace I leave with you; my peace I give to you. Not as the world gives do I give to you. Let not your hearts be troubled, neither let them be afraid."-
John 14:27 (ESV)

Devotional Thought

Your schedule is insane – school, practice, homework, chores, repeat. Your phone won't stop buzzing with drama. Your mind races from one worry to the next. You're living in constant chaos, and everyone expects you to handle it all with a smile. You desperately need peace, but it feels impossibly out of reach in your noisy, demanding world.

Jesus offers a different kind of peace than what the world suggests. The world says peace comes when everything calms down, when problems disappear, when life gets easier. But Jesus gives peace in the middle of the storm. His peace doesn't depend on your circumstances changing; it depends on His presence remaining constant.

This peace isn't just the absence of chaos – it's the presence of Christ. When your world spins out of control, His peace anchors your soul. It's supernatural calm when everything says you should panic. It's the ability to breathe deeply when life feels suffocating. It's knowing that the One who calmed literal storms can certainly calm the storms in your life.

You don't have to manufacture this peace through meditation apps or positive thinking. It's a gift Jesus already gave you. Your job is simply to receive it, to choose His peace over panic, to let His presence be louder than the chaos.

A Prayer for You

Jesus, my life feels so chaotic and overwhelming right now. I need Your supernatural peace that doesn't make sense. Quiet the noise in my mind and help me rest in Your presence. Be my calm in this storm. Let Your peace guard my heart today. Amen.

Your Challenge

Create a "peace pause" routine: When chaos overwhelms you, stop for 60 seconds. Close your eyes, take four slow breaths, and repeat "Jesus, You are my peace" with each exhale. Practice this three times today, even when you're not stressed, so it becomes automatic when you really need it.

Take a Moment

Find the quietest spot you can right now. Sit comfortably and imagine Jesus sitting beside you, completely calm and unhurried. Feel His peaceful presence filling the space around you. Notice how His calm confidence affects your breathing, your heart rate, your racing thoughts. Let His peace be contagious, spreading from Him to you.

Week 16: The Power of Kind Words

God's Truth

"Let no corrupting talk come out of your mouths, but only such as is good for building up, as fits the occasion, that it may give grace to those who hear."–Ephesians 4:29 (ESV)

Devotional Thought

You still remember that cruel comment from middle school. Words that cut deep, left scars, changed how you saw yourself. You've probably also spoken words you wish you could take back – sharp responses to your mom, gossip about that girl, sarcastic comments that went too far. Words seem so small, but their impact is massive.

Your words have incredible power. With them, you can speak life or death, hope or despair, healing or hurt. Every conversation is an opportunity to build someone up or tear them down. That quick comment, text, or social media reply – it all matters more than you realize.

Paul says our words should give grace to those who hear. Imagine if every word you spoke was a gift of grace. Not fake positivity or empty compliments, but genuine words that remind people of their worth, potential, and belovedness. Your encouraging word might be the only kind thing someone hears today.

In a world full of criticism, comparison, and cruelty, your kind words are revolutionary. They're not just nice; they're necessary. That girl everyone gossips about needs your defending words. Your stressed-out friend needs your encouraging text. Your family needs your grateful words. You have the power to change someone's entire day with one kind sentence.

A Prayer for You

God, help me use my words to build others up, not tear them down. When I'm tempted to gossip, complain, or criticize, remind me of the power I hold. Let my words be gifts of grace that point people to You. Make me generous with encouragement. Amen.

Your Challenge

Send three genuine, specific encouragements today – one text, one face-to-face comment, and one social media message. Don't just say "you're awesome." Point out something specific you appreciate about each person. Watch how your intentional kindness creates ripples of positivity that spread further than you can see.

Take a Moment

Think about the kindest words anyone ever spoke to you – words that still encourage you today. Feel the warmth of those words again. Now imagine being the person who gives someone else that same gift. Picture their face lighting up, their shoulders straightening, their confidence growing. You have that power in your mouth right now.

Week 17: When Doubts Shake Your Faith

God's Truth

"Immediately the father of the child cried out and said, 'I believe; help my unbelief!'"–Mark 9:24 (ESV)

Devotional Thought

You sit in youth group hearing everyone talk about their powerful God encounters while you wonder if you've ever truly heard Him. You pray but question if anyone's listening. You see suffering and wonder how a good God allows it. These doubts make you feel like a fake Christian, like everyone else has solid faith while yours crumbles at the slightest challenge.

Here's liberating truth: doubt doesn't disqualify you from faith. The father in Mark's story brought his honest doubt directly to Jesus, and Jesus didn't reject him. Instead, He performed a miracle. Your doubts don't shock God or make Him love you less. He's big enough to handle your hardest questions, your deepest struggles, your most persistent uncertainties.

Faith isn't the absence of doubt – it's choosing to trust despite doubt. It's saying "I believe; help my unbelief" and knowing that's enough. Every biblical hero had moments of doubt. Abraham, Moses, David, Peter – they all questioned, wondered, and wrestled with God. Their faith was refined through doubt, not ruined by it.

Your questions might actually indicate growing faith, not failing faith. You're thinking deeply, refusing to settle for shallow answers. God honors that honest searching. Keep bringing your doubts to Him. He's not intimidated by them.

A Prayer for You

God, I'm struggling to believe right now. My doubts feel bigger than my faith. Help my unbelief. Show me You're real, that You care, that You're working even when I can't see it. Thank You for being patient with my questions. Strengthen my faith through this season. Amen.

Your Challenge

This week, find one trusted adult believer and share one specific doubt you're wrestling with. Don't pretend everything's fine. Have an honest conversation about faith and doubt. You'll likely discover they've had similar struggles and can offer perspective that helps. Authentic community grows when we're honest about our struggles.

Take a Moment

Hold something small but heavy in your hand – a rock, a book, your phone. Feel its weight. Now remember that faith as small as a mustard seed can move mountains. Your faith might feel tiny and insignificant, but God says it's enough. Even microscopic faith, mixed with God's power, can do impossible things.

Week 18: Building Strong and Lasting Friendships

God's Truth

"Two are better than one, because they have a good reward for their toil. For if they fall, one will lift up his fellow. But woe to him who is alone when he falls and has not another to lift him up!"–
Ecclesiastes 4:9-10 (ESV)

Devotional Thought

You've been burned by friendship before – the betrayal, the gossip, the slow drift apart. Now you keep people at arm's length, afraid to fully trust again. Or maybe you have lots of surface friendships but crave something deeper, someone who really knows you. Building lasting friendships feels complicated, especially when everyone seems to already have their person.

God designed you for community, for deep connection with others. Those surface-level friendships that never go beyond small talk? They're not enough. You need friends who will pick you up when you fall, celebrate when you succeed, and stick around when you're not fun to be with. But here's the secret: to have that friend, you must be that friend.

Strong friendships aren't built on perfect people never hurting each other. They're built on forgiveness, honesty, and commitment to work through the messy stuff. They require vulnerability – letting someone see your real struggles, not just your highlight reel. They demand investment – making time when you're busy, listening when you'd rather talk.

The friendships worth having are worth fighting for. They won't just happen; they're intentionally built through countless small moments of choosing to show up, reach out, and care deeply. Start building that foundation today.

A Prayer for You

God, I long for deep, authentic friendships. Help me be the kind of friend I want to have. Give me courage to be vulnerable and wisdom to choose friends wisely. Bring people into my life who will sharpen me and walk with me through every season. Amen.

Your Challenge

Choose one friendship you want to deepen. This week, initiate three intentional connections: suggest a real hangout (not just texting), ask a meaningful question about their life, and share something vulnerable about yourself. Deep friendship requires someone going first – let it be you. Watch how intentionality transforms surface friendship into something real.

Take a Moment

Picture your ideal friendship – how it feels, how you support each other, the memories you create. Now imagine yourself being exactly that kind of friend to someone else. See yourself listening without judgment, showing up when it's inconvenient, celebrating their wins without jealousy. The friendship you're envisioning starts with the friend you choose to be.

Week 19: Breaking Free from Approval Addiction

God's Truth

"For am I now seeking the approval of man, or of God? Or am I trying to please man? If I were still trying to please man, I would not be a servant of Christ."–Galatians 1:10 (ESV)

Devotional Thought

You change your opinion to match the room. You obsess over whether that text sounded weird. You replay conversations, analyzing if everyone liked you. This exhausting performance never ends because there's always another person to impress, another group to fit into. You've become addicted to approval, and the withdrawal symptoms when you don't get it are brutal.

Paul faced a choice: seek human approval or serve Christ. He couldn't do both, and neither can you. When you're constantly shapeshifting to earn everyone's approval, you lose yourself. You become a collection of what others want rather than who God created. This addiction to approval is actually stealing your identity, your peace, and your purpose.

Here's the freedom: God already approves of you. Before you achieved anything, before you impressed anyone, before you proved your worth – He chose you, loved you, approved of you. His opinion is the only one that ultimately matters, and it's already settled in your favor.

Breaking free from approval addiction doesn't mean not caring about others. It means caring more about God's voice than the crowd's applause. It means being kind but not controlled by others' opinions. It means finding your worth in being God's daughter, not in being everyone's favorite.

A Prayer for You

God, I'm exhausted from trying to make everyone happy. Break my addiction to human approval. Help me care more about what You think than what they think. Give me courage to be myself, even if that means some people won't approve. Let Your approval be enough. Amen.

Your Challenge

This week, do one thing you believe is right but might not be popular – speak up for someone, decline an invitation that compromises your values, or share an unpopular opinion with grace. Notice how surviving others' disapproval actually strengthens you. Practice finding your worth in God's approval alone, not in people's reactions.

Take a Moment

Stand in a power pose – feet shoulder-width apart, hands on hips, chin up. Feel the strength in this posture. This is how God sees you – strong, confident, approved. You don't need to shrink yourself to fit others' expectations. Hold this pose for thirty seconds and remember: you're already approved by the King of kings.

Week 20: Discovering Your Spiritual Gifts

God's Truth

"As each has received a gift, use it to serve one another, as good stewards of God's varied grace."–1 Peter 4:10 (ESV)

Devotional Thought

You watch that girl lead worship and wish you had her gift. Another friend seems to always know the right Bible verse for every situation. Someone else has incredible faith for healing prayer. You wonder if God forgot to give you a spiritual gift, if maybe you're just ordinary while everyone else got something special.

But Peter says "each has received a gift" – that includes you. God didn't skip you in the spiritual gift distribution. You have something unique to offer the body of Christ, something that might seem so natural to you that you don't recognize it as a gift. Maybe it's your ability to make newcomers feel welcome, your heart for justice, or your gift of encouragement.

Your spiritual gift might not look like anyone else's, and that's exactly the point. God's grace is varied, expressed through different people in beautifully diverse ways. Your gift might be teaching children, organizing events, showing mercy to outcasts, or having unusual faith for impossible situations. It might be hospitality, wisdom, or the ability to see potential in others.

The key isn't comparing gifts but stewarding yours well. God entrusted you with something specific to serve others. Don't bury it because it seems small or different. Use it. Develop it. Watch how God multiplies your offering.

A Prayer for You

God, help me discover and develop the spiritual gifts You've given me. Show me how You've uniquely equipped me to serve others. Give me courage to use my gifts even when I feel inadequate. Help me steward well what You've entrusted to me. Use me for Your glory. Amen.

Your Challenge

This week, ask three people who know you well what gifts they see in you – what comes naturally to you that blesses others? Often others can see our gifts more clearly than we can. Then find one small way to intentionally use that gift this week to serve someone else.

Take a Moment

Imagine Jesus handing you a wrapped gift with your name on it. See His excitement as you open it, His joy in what He's chosen specifically for you. This gift isn't for you to hide or hoard – it's meant to be shared. Picture yourself using this gift and see how it brings light to dark places.

Week 21: Facing Rejection with Grace

God's Truth

"He was despised and rejected by men, a man of sorrows and acquainted with grief; and as one from whom men hide their faces he was despised, and we esteemed him not."–Isaiah 53:3 (ESV)

Devotional Thought

The friend group that suddenly excluded you. The team you didn't make. The invitation that never came. The relationship that ended. Rejection feels like a punch to the soul, making you question your worth, your likability, everything about yourself. You replay what you could've done differently, wondering why you weren't enough.

Jesus understands rejection more intimately than anyone. He was despised, rejected, betrayed by close friends, denied by those He came to save. The Creator of the universe knows what it feels like to be unwanted. This means when rejection crushes you, you're not crying alone. Jesus is right there, understanding every tear, every hurt, every question of "why not me?"

Rejection doesn't mean you're not valuable – sometimes it means you weren't meant for that space. That closed door might be God's protection, redirection, or preparation for something better. The friends who rejected you might not have the capacity to appreciate who you're becoming. The opportunity you lost might have derailed God's better plan.

Facing rejection with grace doesn't mean pretending it doesn't hurt. It means letting yourself grieve while trusting God to heal and redirect. It means forgiving those who rejected you and refusing to let their opinion define your worth.

A Prayer for You

Jesus, this rejection hurts so deeply. Thank You for understanding this pain personally. Help me forgive those who rejected me and trust that You're working this for good. Heal my heart and show me that Your acceptance matters more than anyone's rejection. Give me grace to move forward. Amen.

Your Challenge

This week, reach out to someone else who might be feeling rejected or left out. Include them, encourage them, or simply let them know they're seen. Sometimes the best way to heal from rejection is to ensure someone else doesn't feel alone. Transform your pain into compassion for others.

Take a Moment

Picture Jesus experiencing rejection – friends running away, crowds turning against Him, being misunderstood and unwanted. Now see Him looking at you with complete understanding, no judgment, just compassion. He chose to endure rejection so you'd never be ultimately rejected by God. Feel His acceptance washing over you, more powerful than any human rejection.

Week 22: Living with Honesty and Integrity

God's Truth

"Whoever walks in integrity walks securely, but he who makes his ways crooked will be found out."-Proverbs 10:9 (ESV)

Devotional Thought

The little lie to avoid getting in trouble. The exaggerated story to sound more interesting. The copied homework you claim as your own. The different versions of yourself you present to different people. These seem like survival tactics in high school, but they're actually creating an exhausting web that gets harder to maintain. You're constantly anxious about being found out, keeping stories straight, maintaining facades.

Integrity means being the same person in every room, with every group, in every situation. It's telling the truth even when lies would be easier. It's doing the right thing even when no one's watching. This isn't about being perfect – it's about being genuine, admitting mistakes, and choosing honesty even when it costs something.

Walking in integrity brings incredible freedom. You never have to remember which version of the truth you told. You can look people in the eye without shame. You sleep peacefully knowing you have nothing to hide. Yes, honesty might sometimes lead to consequences, but those consequences are better than the prison of deception.

When you live with integrity, you walk securely. Not because life becomes easy, but because you're building on a foundation that won't crumble. Your reputation, relationships, and self-respect remain intact.

A Prayer for You

God, help me choose honesty even when it's hard. Give me courage to live with integrity in a world that often rewards deception. When I'm tempted to lie or compromise, remind me that truth brings freedom. Help me be the same authentic person everywhere I go. Amen.

Your Challenge

This week, practice radical honesty in small ways. Admit when you don't understand something instead of pretending. Acknowledge mistakes immediately instead of covering them up. Tell the truth about why you're really upset. Notice how honesty, though sometimes uncomfortable initially, actually strengthens your relationships and self-respect.

Take a Moment

Think about how exhausting it is to maintain lies or false versions of yourself. Feel that weight on your shoulders. Now imagine setting down that heavy burden, walking away free and light. That's what integrity offers – the freedom to be exactly who you are without apology or pretense. Breathe in that freedom right now.

Week 23: The Courage to Be Different

God's Truth

"Do not be conformed to this world, but be transformed by the renewal of your mind, that by testing you may discern what is the will of God, what is good and acceptable and perfect."–Romans 12:2 (ESV)

Devotional Thought

Everyone's doing it, watching it, wearing it, saying it. The pressure to conform feels crushing, like standing out would be social suicide. You want to follow Jesus, but you also want friends. You want to honor God, but you also want to fit in. This tension tears at you daily, making you feel like you're constantly choosing between your faith and your social life.

God isn't calling you to be weird for weirdness' sake. He's calling you to be transformed, to think differently, to march to heaven's rhythm instead of culture's beat. This might mean saying no when everyone says yes, staying silent when everyone gossips, or standing up when everyone stays seated. It definitely means looking different from the world around you.

Being different isn't about being better than others – it's about being obedient to God. It's choosing His approval over their acceptance. Sometimes this leads to respect from unexpected places. People secretly admire those brave enough to stand for something, even if they won't join you.

The courage to be different isn't mustered up through will-power. It comes from a renewed mind that sees things from God's perspective. When you understand your true identity and purpose, conforming to the world loses its appeal.

A Prayer for You

God, give me courage to stand out when following You means being different. Help me care more about Your will than fitting in. Transform my mind so I naturally desire what You desire. When being different feels lonely, remind me I'm never alone. Make me brave. Amen.

Your Challenge

This week, identify one area where you've been conforming to avoid standing out – maybe it's laughing at inappropriate jokes, staying quiet about your faith, or participating in gossip. Choose to be lovingly different in that area. Don't be preachy, just be consistently, courageously yourself. Watch how God honors your obedience.

Take a Moment

Imagine yourself as a light in a dark room. You stand out not because you're trying to be seen, but because light naturally contrasts darkness. You're not different to judge others but to show them another way is possible. Feel the warmth of that light within you – that's God's presence making you beautifully different.

Week 24: When Faith Feels Distant

God's Truth

"My God, my God, why have you forsaken me? Why are you so far from saving me, from the words of my groaning?"–Psalm 22:1 (ESV)

Devotional Thought

You used to feel God so clearly – during worship, in prayer, reading Scripture. But now? Nothing. Your prayers feel like they're bouncing off the ceiling. Worship feels mechanical. The Bible seems like just words on a page. You wonder if you did something wrong, if God gave up on you, if maybe your faith was never real. This spiritual desert feels endless and frightening.

Even David, a man after God's own heart, felt abandoned by God. Even Jesus quoted this very psalm on the cross. Feeling distant from God doesn't mean you are distant from God. Feelings aren't always facts. Sometimes God feels far because He's teaching you to walk by faith, not by feelings.

These dry seasons often come right before breakthrough. They're not punishment but preparation. God is developing deeper roots in you, teaching you to seek Him for who He is, not just for how He makes you feel. He's still there, still working, still loving you, even when you can't sense it.

Your faith is being refined from emotion-based to trust-based. This isn't a step backward but a leap forward into mature faith that can weather any storm. Keep showing up. Keep seeking.

The feeling will return, but the faith you're building now will last forever.

A Prayer for You

God, I can't feel You right now and it scares me. Help me trust that You're still here even when my emotions say otherwise. Strengthen my faith beyond feelings. Show me You're working even in this silence. I choose to believe You're near even when You feel far. Amen.

Your Challenge

This week, do three faith actions despite not feeling it: worship even without emotion, pray even without sensing response, serve even without spiritual highs. Act on what you know to be true rather than what you feel. Faith is a choice, not a feeling. Choose faith and watch feelings eventually follow.

Take a Moment

Hold your breath for ten seconds. Feel that desperate need for air. Now breathe deeply. Sometimes God removes the feeling of His presence like holding spiritual breath – not to hurt you but to make you treasure the next breath of His presence even more. Trust that this distance is temporary and purposeful.

Week 25: Embracing the Story God Is Writing

God's Truth

"And we know that for those who love God all things work together for good, for those who are called according to his purpose."-Romans 8:28 (ESV)

Devotional Thought

Your story isn't turning out like you planned. The family situation you'd never choose. The struggle you can't seem to overcome. The loss that changed everything. You look at other girls' stories – their intact families, their natural talents, their easier paths – and wonder why your story includes so much hard. It feels unfair, like God is writing a tragedy while giving everyone else a fairy tale.

But God is the master storyteller, and He doesn't write boring stories. Every plot twist, even the painful ones, is purposeful. That difficulty you wish you could delete? It's developing strength others will desperately need from you. That mess in your past? It's becoming a message of hope. That brokenness? It's where God's light shines brightest.

Romans 8:28 doesn't promise all things are good, but that God works them together for good. Like ingredients that taste terrible alone but create something delicious when combined, your story's hard parts are being woven into something beautiful. You can't see the full picture yet because you're still in the middle chapters.

Your story isn't meant to be compared to others' stories. It's uniquely yours, perfectly designed to display God's glory through your life. Embrace it – the good, the hard, the unexpected.

A Prayer for You

God, help me trust the story You're writing with my life. When I want to rewrite the hard parts, remind me You're the perfect author. Give me faith to believe You're working everything together for good, even when I can't see it yet. Help me embrace my unique story. Amen.

Your Challenge

This week, share one difficult part of your story with someone who might need hope. Don't minimize the pain, but share how God is working through it. Your vulnerability about your story's hard chapters might be exactly what someone needs to hear. Your mess can become someone else's message of hope.

Take a Moment

Imagine your life as a book God is writing. See Him carefully crafting each chapter, some with tears, some with laughter, all with purpose. Notice how the difficult chapters make the beautiful ones even more meaningful. Trust the Author – He knows how to write a story worth reading, and yours isn't finished yet.

Week 26: The Beauty of Waiting Well

God's Truth

"Wait for the Lord; be strong, and let your heart take courage; wait for the Lord!"–Psalm 27:14 (ESV)

Devotional Thought

Waiting for test results. Waiting for that relationship. Waiting for clarity about your future. Waiting for prayers to be answered. Everyone tells you to be patient, but waiting feels like torture when everyone else seems to be moving forward while you're stuck in place. You wonder if God forgot about you, if maybe you're doing something wrong, if this waiting will ever end.

The psalmist doesn't just say "wait" – he says "be strong, and let your heart take courage." Waiting isn't passive; it's active. It takes strength to wait well, courage to trust God's timing over your demands. Waiting well means growing while you wait, preparing for what's coming, becoming who you need to be for the next season.

Think about a seed underground. It's not just sitting there; it's developing roots, gathering strength, preparing to burst through the soil. Your waiting season is your root-developing season. The deeper the roots, the taller the tree can grow. God isn't making you wait to be cruel; He's ensuring you're ready for what He's preparing.

Waiting well means worshiping before you see the answer, thanking God in advance, staying faithful in the meantime. It's choosing to believe that God's delays are not His denials. This waiting is forming patience, faith, and character that rushing would rob from you.

A Prayer for You

Lord, waiting is so hard, and I'm struggling to be patient. Give me strength and courage to wait well. Help me grow during this season instead of just enduring it. Show me what You're developing in me through this waiting. I trust Your timing over mine. Amen.

Your Challenge

Create a "waiting well" routine: Each day this week, do something productive toward your future while you wait – learn a skill, strengthen a relationship, deepen your faith. Document what you're learning in this season. When your waiting ends, you'll see how God used this time to prepare you perfectly.

Take a Moment

Picture a master chef preparing an elaborate meal. Some ingredients cook quickly, others need hours to develop their flavor. Rushing would ruin the masterpiece. God is the master chef of your life, knowing exactly how long each season needs. Trust His timing – He's creating something worth waiting for.

Week 27: Learning to Forgive Yourself

God's Truth

"Therefore, there is now no condemnation for those who are in Christ Jesus."–Romans 8:1 (ESV)

Devotional Thought

You've replayed that mistake a thousand times. Every night, shame whispers reminders of what you did, who you hurt, how you failed. You've asked God for forgiveness repeatedly, but you can't seem to forgive yourself. It's like you're punishing yourself, believing you deserve to carry this guilt forever. Everyone else seems to have moved on, but you're still stuck in that moment.

Here's what's actually happening: you're holding yourself to a higher standard than God does. If the Creator of the universe says there's no condemnation for you, who are you to condemn yourself? You're not more righteous than God. Your refusal to forgive yourself isn't humility – it's actually pride, believing your judgment matters more than His.

Self-forgiveness isn't saying what you did was okay. It's accepting God's forgiveness and agreeing with His verdict over your life. When you refuse to forgive yourself, you're essentially telling Jesus His sacrifice wasn't enough. But it was enough. It covered that mistake, that sin, that regret you can't let go of.

Learning to forgive yourself is a process. It means catching those condemning thoughts and replacing them with God's truth. It means treating yourself with the same grace you'd offer a friend. It means moving forward, knowing you're forgiven, free, and loved.

A Prayer for You

God, I know You've forgiven me, but I can't seem to forgive myself. Help me see myself through Your eyes of grace. Break these chains of self-condemnation. Teach me to accept Your forgiveness fully and walk in the freedom You've already given me. Thank You for Your complete forgiveness. Amen.

Your Challenge

When self-condemning thoughts arise this week, stop and say out loud: "There is no condemnation for me because I am in Christ Jesus." Say it three times, each time with more conviction. Then do something kind for yourself – something you'd do for a friend who needed grace and encouragement.

Take a Moment

Place both hands over your heart. Feel it beating steadily, constantly, faithfully. That's how God's forgiveness works – constant, never failing, always available. With each heartbeat, imagine God's forgiveness pumping through your entire being, cleansing every cell, every memory, every regret. You are completely, thoroughly, permanently forgiven.

Week 28: When Everyone Else Seems Perfect

God's Truth

"Not that I have already obtained this or am already perfect, but I press on to make it my own, because Christ Jesus has made me his own."–
Philippians 3:12 (ESV)

Devotional Thought

Scroll through social media and everyone's life looks flawless. She has perfect skin, perfect grades, perfect family, perfect faith. You look at your life – the acne, the B's and C's, the family drama, the spiritual struggles – and feel like you're failing at everything. Everyone else seems to have it all together while you're barely holding on. This comparison makes you feel defeated before you even start your day.

Even Paul, who wrote much of the New Testament, admitted he wasn't perfect. He was still pressing on, still growing, still becoming. If Paul wasn't perfect, why do you expect yourself to be? Those "perfect" people you're comparing yourself to? They're fighting battles you know nothing about, hiding struggles behind their smiles, dealing with insecurities just like you.

Nobody posts their failures, their arguments, their anxiety attacks. Social media is everyone's highlight reel, not their behind-the-scenes reality. That girl with perfect skin? She might cry herself to sleep from loneliness. The straight-A student? She might be crumbling under pressure. Perfect doesn't exist – it's an illusion that keeps you from appreciating your own journey.

God isn't asking for perfection; He's asking for progress. Press on, like Paul said. Keep growing, keep trying, keep becoming who God created you to be.

A Prayer for You

God, I'm exhausted from comparing myself to everyone's perfect facade. Help me remember that nobody has it all together. Show me that You're not disappointed in my imperfection but delighted in my progress. Help me focus on my own journey instead of everyone else's highlight reel. Amen.

Your Challenge

This week, unfollow or mute three social media accounts that trigger comparison and feelings of inadequacy. Replace them with accounts that inspire genuine growth, share real struggles, or point you toward God. Notice how curating your input changes your outlook. You control what influences you – choose wisely.

Take a Moment

Look at your hands. Notice they're not perfectly symmetrical – one might be slightly larger, fingers slightly different. Yet they work together perfectly to accomplish everything you need. Your imperfections don't disqualify you from purpose. God uses imperfect people because that's the only kind there is. Embrace your beautiful imperfection.

Week 29: Gratitude Changes Everything

God's Truth

"Give thanks in all circumstances; for this is the will of God in Christ Jesus for you."–1 Thessalonians 5:18 (ESV)

Devotional Thought

Your phone screen cracked. Your crush likes someone else. Your parents are being impossible. It's easy to list everything going wrong, to focus on what you lack, to complain about life's unfairness. Negativity feels natural, almost automatic. But what if there's a practice so powerful it could completely shift your perspective, your mood, even your circumstances? That practice is gratitude.

Notice Paul doesn't say give thanks FOR all circumstances, but IN all circumstances. You don't have to be grateful for the hard things, but you can find something to be grateful for during them. That cracked phone? You still have a phone. That crush situation? You're learning what you really want in a relationship. Those impossible parents? They care enough to have rules.

Gratitude literally rewires your brain. It shifts your focus from what's missing to what's present, from problems to provisions. It's not toxic positivity or pretending everything's fine. It's choosing to acknowledge good even when bad exists. It's recognizing God's faithfulness even in difficult seasons.

When gratitude becomes your default response, everything changes. Complaints transform into contentment. Bitterness melts into blessing. Problems shrink when placed next to provisions. This isn't just positive thinking – it's spiritual warfare against discontentment, comparison, and despair.

A Prayer for You

God, help me develop eyes that see reasons for gratitude everywhere. When I'm tempted to complain, remind me of Your countless blessings. Teach me to give thanks in all circumstances, trusting that gratitude will shift my perspective and draw me closer to You. Thank You for everything, especially what I take for granted. Amen.

Your Challenge

Start a "gratitude alarm" on your phone for three random times daily. When it goes off, immediately name three specific things you're grateful for in that moment – not generic things, but specific, present blessings. Watch how this simple practice shifts your entire day's trajectory toward joy.

Take a Moment

Look around you right now and find five things you usually ignore but couldn't live without – oxygen, electricity, clean water, a roof, clothes. Spend ten seconds appreciating each one. Feel how gratitude for simple things creates warmth in your chest. That warmth is joy growing from thankfulness. Gratitude literally changes how you feel.

Week 30: Understanding and Managing Emotions

God's Truth

"Be angry and do not sin; do not let the sun go down on your anger."-Ephesians 4:26 (ESV)

Devotional Thought

One moment you're fine, the next you're sobbing over something small. Your emotions feel like a rollercoaster you didn't choose to ride – intense, unpredictable, overwhelming. Adults tell you it's "just hormones," but that doesn't make the feelings less real. You wonder if you're too emotional, too sensitive, too much. Sometimes you feel everything; sometimes you feel nothing. Both extremes feel wrong.

God gave you emotions – all of them. Even Jesus experienced anger, sadness, frustration, and joy. Emotions aren't sinful; they're signals. Anger might signal injustice. Sadness might signal loss. Anxiety might signal you need to slow down. The key isn't eliminating emotions but understanding and managing them wisely.

Paul says be angry but don't sin. Feel the emotion, but don't let it control your actions. You can feel hurt without hurting others. You can feel angry without exploding. You can feel sad without isolating. Emotions are meant to inform you, not control you. They're valid visitors, but terrible masters.

Managing emotions doesn't mean suppressing them. It means acknowledging them, understanding their message, and choosing your response. It means taking them to God, who understands every feeling you experience. Your emotions don't make you weak – they make you human.

A Prayer for You

God, my emotions feel so overwhelming and confusing. Help me understand what they're trying to tell me. Give me wisdom to feel without sinning, to express without exploding. Teach me to bring every emotion to You. Thank You for creating me with the capacity to feel deeply. Amen.

Your Challenge

This week, when intense emotions hit, practice the "NAME IT, CLAIM IT, TAME IT" method: NAME the emotion specifically, CLAIM it without judgment ("I'm feeling anxious"), TAME it with one healthy response (deep breathing, prayer, walking). This simple process puts you back in control instead of being controlled by emotions.

Take a Moment

Put your hand on your stomach and breathe deeply five times. With each breath, imagine you're creating space between yourself and your emotions. You are not your emotions – you're experiencing them. Like clouds passing through the sky, emotions move through you but don't define you. Feel the space, the calm beneath the storm.

Week 31: Setting Healthy Boundaries

God's Truth

"Above all else, guard your heart, for everything you do flows from it."–Proverbs 4:23 (ESV)

Devotional Thought

She always dumps her drama on you but never listens to yours. He keeps pushing physical boundaries you've already set. Your family expects you to be available 24/7. You feel guilty saying no, so you say yes to everything until you're exhausted, resentful, and empty. You wonder if having boundaries makes you selfish, mean, or un-Christian. After all, aren't you supposed to love everyone and turn the other cheek?

Guarding your heart isn't about building walls – it's about installing gates. Gates that open for the right things and close to protect you from harm. Jesus, the perfect example of love, had boundaries. He withdrew from crowds, said no to certain requests, and removed Himself from toxic situations. If Jesus had boundaries, you need them too.

Boundaries aren't about punishing others; they're about protecting yourself. They're not walls that say "I don't care" but gates that say "I care about both of us enough to keep this healthy." When you don't set boundaries, resentment grows, relationships suffer, and you lose yourself trying to be everything to everyone.

Healthy boundaries might disappoint some people, and that's okay. The right people will respect your boundaries. The wrong people will reveal themselves by fighting them.

A Prayer for You

God, give me wisdom to know what boundaries I need and courage to set them. Help me guard my heart without hardening it. Show me how to love others while still protecting my peace. When people push against my boundaries, give me strength to hold firm in love. Amen.

Your Challenge

Identify one area where you need a boundary – maybe it's phone time, physical touch, or emotional availability. This week, communicate that boundary clearly to someone: "I care about you, AND I need..." Practice holding that boundary even when it feels uncomfortable. Remember, discomfort now prevents resentment later.

Take a Moment

Imagine your heart as a beautiful garden. Without a fence, anyone can trample the flowers, steal the fruit, or plant weeds. Now picture a lovely fence with a gate – it protects the beauty while still allowing chosen people to enter and enjoy. That's what boundaries do – they protect your inner garden while maintaining healthy connections.

Week 32: Finding Joy in Loneliness

God's Truth

"Turn to me and be gracious to me, for I am lonely and afflicted."–Psalm 25:16 (ESV)

Devotional Thought

Friday night, everyone's out, and you're alone in your room. Not because you chose solitude, but because loneliness chose you. The silence feels heavy, social media makes it worse, and you wonder if anyone would notice if you disappeared. Loneliness aches differently than other pain – it's an emptiness that feels consuming, a disconnect that makes you question your worth.

David, surrounded by people as king, still felt lonely and afflicted. Even with a palace full of servants, he experienced that hollow feeling you know so well. But notice what he did – he turned to God. He didn't pretend everything was fine or numb the feeling with distractions. He brought his loneliness directly to God.

Here's the secret: loneliness isn't the absence of people; it's feeling unknown. You can feel lonely in a crowded room if no one really sees you. But God sees you, knows you, and is with you right now in your loneliness. He's not just present; He's gracious, tender, understanding exactly how you feel.

Sometimes God allows loneliness to draw you closer to Him, to teach you that He's enough, to prepare you for deeper relationships. Loneliness doesn't mean you're unloved or forgotten. It might mean God wants some one-on-one time with His daughter.

A Prayer for You

God, this loneliness hurts so much. Thank You for understanding this feeling and never leaving me truly alone. Help me find joy in Your presence when human company is absent. Show me how to transform lonely moments into intimate encounters with You. Fill this emptiness with Your love. Amen.

Your Challenge

This week, when loneliness hits, instead of scrolling through others' social lives, do something that connects you to God or yourself: dance to worship music, create art, prayer-walk your neighborhood, or learn something new. Transform loneliness from something that happens to you into something productive that happens for you.

Take a Moment

Sit quietly and imagine Jesus sitting right beside you in your loneliness. He's not checking His phone or distracted – He's fully present with you. Feel His companionship, His complete attention, His delight in simply being with you. You might be alone by human standards, but you're never truly alone. His presence changes everything.

Week 33: Your Body Is a Gift from God

God's Truth

"Or do you not know that your body is a temple of the Holy Spirit within you, whom you have from God? You are not your own, for you were bought with a price. So glorify God in your body."–1 Corinthians 6:19-20 (ESV)

Devotional Thought

You critique every inch in the mirror. Too much here, not enough there. You compare your body to filtered images, impossible standards, and everyone else who seems more beautiful. Maybe you punish your body with extreme diets, harm it with destructive habits, or simply hate it for not looking like you wish it would. The relationship with your body feels like a war you're constantly losing.

But your body isn't your enemy – it's a temple. Not a temple you built, but one God carefully designed to house His Spirit. Every feature you criticize, God intentionally chose. Your body isn't a mistake or a rough draft; it's exactly the temple God wanted to create. He doesn't make errors.

This temple has carried you through every moment of your life. It allows you to hug friends, dance to music, taste amazing food, see sunsets. Your body is the vehicle through which you love others, serve God, and experience life. It deserves gratitude, not hatred; care, not punishment.

Glorifying God in your body doesn't mean achieving perfection. It means treating your body with respect, nourishing it well, and using it for God's purposes. It means seeing your body as God sees it – not an object to perfect, but a gift to steward.

A Prayer for You

God, help me see my body as You do – a temple, a gift, a miraculous creation. Heal my relationship with my body. When I'm tempted to hate or harm it, remind me it houses Your Spirit. Teach me to glorify You by caring for this temple You've given me. Amen.

Your Challenge

This week, thank your body for three specific things it does for you each day – maybe your legs for carrying you, your arms for hugging, your eyes for seeing beauty. Shift focus from how your body looks to what it does. Gratitude for function often heals frustration with form.

Take a Moment

Stand up and stretch your arms wide. Feel your muscles working, your lungs breathing, your heart beating. This incredible machine performs thousands of functions without you even thinking about it. Marvel at the miracle of your body – not its appearance, but its faithful service to you every single day. Your body is amazing.

Week 34: When Dreams Don't Work Out

God's Truth

"Many are the plans in the mind of a man, but it is the purpose of the Lord that will stand."–Proverbs 19:21 (ESV)

Devotional Thought

You didn't make the team you trained for all year. The college you dreamed about rejected you. The relationship you thought was forever ended abruptly. That opportunity you prayed for went to someone else. Your carefully planned future just crumbled, and you're left wondering if dreams are even worth having. The disappointment feels crushing, like failure, like you'll never recover from this setback.

Your plans seemed perfect, but God's purpose is better – even when it doesn't feel that way. That closed door isn't God's rejection; it's His redirection. He sees the full map while you only see the next turn. What looks like a dead end to you might be God protecting you from a road that would've led somewhere harmful.

Joseph's dream of greatness seemed destroyed when his brothers sold him into slavery. But God used that betrayal to position Joseph to save nations. Your disrupted dream might be the very path to your greater purpose. God isn't ruining your story; He's editing it for a better ending than you could write yourself.

Dreams aren't wrong, but hold them loosely. Let God reshape, redirect, or even replace them with something better. His purpose will stand, and it's always better than your best plan.

A Prayer for You

God, this broken dream hurts so much. I don't understand why You allowed this door to close. Help me trust that Your purpose is better than my plans. Give me courage to dream again and wisdom to hold those dreams with open hands. Show me the new direction You're leading. Amen.

Your Challenge

This week, think of one dream that didn't work out in the past that you're now grateful for. Share this story with someone who's facing disappointment. Then identify one small step toward a new dream or adjusted dream. Failed dreams aren't the end – they're often the beginning of something better.

Take a Moment

Hold something fragile in your hands – maybe a flower or delicate object. Notice how you can hold it firmly enough to keep it safe but gently enough not to crush it. This is how to hold dreams – secure but not strangling, valued but not worshipped. Practice holding dreams with open hands.

Week 35: Strength in Vulnerability

God's Truth

"Therefore, confess your sins to one another and pray for one another, that you may be healed." — James 5:16 (ESV)

Devotional Thought

You've built walls so high that no one can hurt you – but no one can truly know you either. You wear masks of having it all together, terrified that if people saw the real you, they'd leave. Vulnerability feels like weakness, like giving people ammunition to wound you. So you stay surface-level, safe but disconnected, protected but lonely.

But Paul discovered something revolutionary: weakness isn't something to hide but something to boast about. When you're vulnerable about your struggles, fears, and failures, you create space for God's power to shine. Your vulnerability doesn't push people away; it draws the right people closer. It gives others permission to be real too.

Think about the people you trust most. They're probably not the ones who seem perfect but the ones who've shared their imperfections with you. Vulnerability creates connection that perfection never could. When you say "I'm struggling," you might discover others saying "me too" instead of judging you.

Vulnerability isn't oversharing with everyone or having no boundaries. It's strategically choosing to be real with safe people. It's admitting you need help, saying you're not okay, asking for prayer. This kind of strength looks like weakness to the world, but it's actually courage in its purest form.

A Prayer for You

God, being vulnerable terrifies me. Help me find safe people to be real with. Give me courage to admit weakness, knowing Your power shows up strongest there. Break down walls that keep me isolated. Show me that vulnerability is strength, not weakness. Help me be brave enough to be seen. Amen.

Your Challenge

This week, be vulnerable with one trusted person about something you usually hide. Maybe it's a fear, a struggle, or a prayer request. Start small if needed, but take the risk of being known. Notice how vulnerability, though scary at first, often leads to deeper connection and unexpected support.

Take a Moment

Press your palms together in front of your chest, then slowly open them, palms up. Feel how exposed your palms are – vulnerable, open, unable to protect themselves. Yet this is also the position for receiving. Vulnerability feels exposed, but it's the only posture that allows you to receive love, help, and connection.

Week 36: Creating Space for God

God's Truth

"Be still, and know that I am God. I will be exalted among the nations, I will be exalted in the earth!"–Psalm 46:10 (ESV)

Devotional Thought

Your day starts with alarm panic and ends with exhausted collapse. Between school, activities, homework, family, friends, and phone notifications, there's no margin, no breathing room, no space. You want to connect with God, but your schedule is already bursting. You promise you'll pray tomorrow, read your Bible later, worship when things calm down. But they never do.

"Be still" feels impossible in your noisy, demanding world. But God isn't asking for hours – He's asking for intention. Creating space for God doesn't mean adding another task to your overwhelming list. It means recognizing that without Him, all your busyness is just noise. When you're too busy for God, you're too busy.

Stillness isn't just physical; it's mental and emotional. It's turning off notifications for ten minutes. It's choosing worship music over regular playlists. It's praying while walking to class. It's transforming everyday moments into sacred spaces. God doesn't need perfect quiet; He just needs your attention.

When you create space for God, everything else falls into proper perspective. Problems shrink, peace grows, and purpose clarifies. That time you think you don't have for God? He'll multiply it when you give Him the firstfruits of your day.

A Prayer for You

God, my life feels too full for You, and that's backward. Help me create space for You in my daily chaos. Show me what needs to go to make room for what matters most. Teach me to be still enough to know You're God. You deserve the first of my time, not leftovers. Amen.

Your Challenge

This week, create one non-negotiable "God space" in your day – maybe five minutes before you check your phone each morning, or turning your shower into a prayer time. Guard this space fiercely. Don't let anything crowd it out. Notice how even small spaces for God change your entire day.

Take a Moment

Right now, turn off all notifications for just two minutes. Sit in complete stillness. Don't pray with words, just be present with God. Feel your breathing slow, your shoulders relax, your mind quiet. This is what your soul craves – not more activity, but space to simply be with God.

Week 37: When You Feel Forgotten

God's Truth

"Can a woman forget her nursing child, that she should have no compassion on the son of her womb? Even these may forget, yet I will not forget you."–Isaiah 49:15 (ESV)

Devotional Thought

Everyone forgot your birthday. Your prayer seems stuck in God's spam folder. Friends make plans without thinking of you. You feel invisible at school, overlooked at home, forgotten by the world. You watch others get noticed, celebrated, chosen, while you fade into the background. This feeling of being forgotten makes you wonder if you matter at all.

God uses the strongest human bond – a mother's love for her baby – and says His remembrance of you is even stronger. Even if the unthinkable happened and a mother forgot her child, God will never, could never, forget you. You're not just on His mind; you're engraved on His palms. He thinks about you more than you think about yourself.

Being forgotten by people doesn't mean you're forgettable. Sometimes you're in a hidden season where God is developing you privately for public purpose. Joseph was forgotten in prison before becoming second in command. David was overlooked by his family before becoming king. Hidden doesn't mean forgotten.

When you feel invisible, remember God sees you. When you feel overlooked, remember God chose you. When you feel forgotten, remember you're unforgettable to the One who matters most. His attention never wavers.

A Prayer for You

God, I feel so forgotten and invisible right now. Remind me that You see me, know me, and never forget me. When people overlook me, let Your attention be enough. Help me trust that You're working even in hidden seasons. Thank You for thinking of me constantly. I matter to You. Amen.

Your Challenge

This week, notice someone else who seems forgotten or overlooked. Send them an unexpected message, include them in something, or simply acknowledge their presence. Be for someone else the reminder that they're not forgotten. Sometimes healing our own feeling of invisibility comes through making others feel seen.

Take a Moment

Look at your hands, specifically your palms. God says you're engraved on His palms – permanently marked, impossible to forget. Trace your finger across your palm and imagine your name written on God's hands. Every time He moves, He sees you. You're literally unforgettable to Him.

Week 38: The Power of Being Present

God's Truth

"Therefore do not be anxious about tomorrow, for tomorrow will be anxious for itself. Sufficient for the day is its own trouble."–Matthew 6:34 (ESV)

Devotional Thought

You're physically in class but mentally planning tonight. You're with friends but checking your phone constantly. You're at dinner but worried about tomorrow's test. You live everywhere except where you are – either replaying the past or rehearsing the future. This constant mental time travel exhausts you, and you miss the only moment you actually have: right now.

Jesus says tomorrow has enough trouble without you borrowing it today. When you're constantly living in tomorrow's worries or yesterday's regrets, you miss today's blessings. That sunset you didn't notice because you were scrolling. That conversation you half-heard because you were planning. That moment of peace you missed because you were anxious about later.

Being present isn't just mindfulness; it's faithfulness. It's trusting God with your past and future while fully engaging with your present. It's putting your phone down during conversations. It's noticing the small beauties God scattered throughout your day. It's being where you are, fully, completely.

The present is the only place where life actually happens. It's where you meet God, love people, and experience joy. Yesterday is gone, tomorrow isn't guaranteed, but today – this moment – is yours.

A Prayer for You

God, help me stop living in yesterday's regrets and tomorrow's worries. Teach me to be fully present where You've placed me. Help me notice the blessings in this moment instead of always looking ahead or behind. Give me grace to trust You with time and be faithful with now. Amen.

Your Challenge

Practice the "5-minute phone-free" challenge: During each meal this week, put your phone completely away for the first five minutes. Be fully present – taste your food, engage in conversation, notice your surroundings. See how these small moments of presence change your experience and connections with others around you.

Take a Moment

Stop everything and notice five things about this exact moment – the temperature, the sounds, the light, how your body feels, what you can smell. This is your life happening right now. Not on your phone, not in your plans, but right here. God is meeting you in this present moment. Don't miss it.

Week 39: Using Your Influence for Good

God's Truth

"Let no one despise you for your youth, but set the believers an example in speech, in conduct, in love, in faith, in purity."–1 Timothy 4:12 (ESV)

Devotional Thought

You think influence requires thousands of followers, perfect aesthetics, or a platform. You believe you're too young, too ordinary, too unimportant to make a difference. But influence isn't about follower count – it's about impact. You're already influencing someone, whether you realize it or not. That freshman watching how you treat others. Your younger sibling copying your habits. Your friends being shaped by your words.

Paul told Timothy not to let anyone dismiss him because of his age. Your youth doesn't disqualify you from influence; it uniquely positions you for it. You speak the language of your generation. You understand struggles adults might miss. You have access to people who need exactly what you offer.

Being an example doesn't mean being perfect. It means being intentional with your words, actions, love, faith, and purity. It means using your social media to encourage rather than impress. It means standing up for the underdog, speaking truth in love, and showing there's a different way to live.

Your influence might seem small, but God specializes in multiplication. One kind word, one brave stand, one authentic moment can ripple further than you imagine. You don't need a platform to be influential. You just need to be faithful with the influence you already have.

A Prayer for You

God, show me the influence I already have and help me use it wisely. Give me courage to be an example even when I feel inadequate. Help me influence others toward You through my words and actions. Use my life to make a difference, no matter how small it seems. Amen.

Your Challenge

This week, use your influence intentionally in three ways: post something encouraging on social media, defend someone who's being criticized, and invite someone who's usually excluded. Document not for likes but to remind yourself that influence is about impact, not impressiveness. Notice how small acts of positive influence create ripple effects.

Take a Moment

Think of someone who positively influenced your life – maybe without even knowing it. Consider how their example changed you. Now realize you're that person for someone else. Your life is influencing others right now. Feel the weight and privilege of that responsibility. Choose to influence for good.

Week 40: Rest Is Not a Weakness

God's Truth

"Come to me, all who labor and are heavy laden, and I will give you rest. Take my yoke upon you, and learn from me, for I am gentle and lowly in heart, and you will find rest for your souls."–Matthew 11:28-29 (ESV)

Devotional Thought

You wear exhaustion like a badge of honor. Five hours of sleep, three coffees, back-to-back activities – you're proud of how much you can handle. Rest feels lazy, unproductive, like falling behind while everyone else races ahead. You push through exhaustion, ignore your body's signals, and crash only when you absolutely have to. This pace feels normal, even necessary, but it's slowly destroying you.

Jesus doesn't admire your exhaustion; He invites you to rest. Not just physical sleep, but soul rest – the kind that comes from releasing the pressure to constantly perform. He knows you're carrying weights you weren't meant to bear alone. That's why He offers to trade your heavy burden for His light yoke. This isn't about doing nothing; it's about doing life with Him.

Rest isn't weakness; it's wisdom. Even God rested after creation, not because He was tired, but to model rhythm for you. Your body, mind, and spirit need rest to function properly. When you refuse to rest, you're essentially saying you know better than your Creator.

Rest is an act of faith, trusting that God can handle what you're putting down. It's believing you're human, not superhuman.

A Prayer for You

Jesus, I'm so tired but afraid to slow down. Help me see rest as strength, not weakness. Teach me to come to You when I'm overwhelmed instead of pushing harder. Give me wisdom to create rhythms of rest in my life. I trust You to handle what I need to release. Amen.

Your Challenge

This week, schedule one hour of intentional rest – not scrolling or Netflix, but true rest. Take a nap, sit in nature, listen to calming music, or simply be still. Put it in your calendar like an important appointment. Notice how rest actually increases your productivity and peace in other areas.

Take a Moment

Lie down or sit comfortably and progressively relax each part of your body, starting from your toes up to your head. As you release physical tension, imagine also releasing mental and emotional burdens to God. Feel how good it is to let go, to rest, to trust God with the weight you've been carrying.

Week 41: Contentment in a World of Comparison

God's Truth

"But godliness with contentment is great gain, for we brought nothing into the world, and we cannot take anything out of the world."–1 Timothy 6:6-7 (ESV)

Devotional Thought

Everyone has the new phone, the trendy clothes, the perfect life you can't afford. You open social media and immediately feel behind, lacking, not enough. The more you see, the less satisfied you become with your own life. What you have seems embarrassing compared to what they have. This constant wanting is exhausting, expensive, and never-ending because there's always something newer, better, more.

Paul calls contentment with godliness "great gain" – meaning it's actually wealth to be satisfied with what you have. This doesn't mean settling for less or not having goals. It means recognizing that more stuff won't fill the emptiness. That designer bag won't make you more valuable. That perfect aesthetic won't bring lasting happiness.

Contentment is rebellious in a culture that profits from your dissatisfaction. It's choosing gratitude over greed, enough over excess. It's realizing that everything you're chasing can't come with you to eternity anyway. The girl with everything might be desperately unhappy, while you have riches she can't buy – peace, purpose, genuine relationships.

When you practice contentment, comparison loses its power. You stop measuring your life against others and start appreciating your unique blessings. This isn't about having less ambition; it's about finding satisfaction in what truly matters.

A Prayer for You

God, I'm tired of always wanting more and never feeling satisfied. Teach me contentment in this comparison-obsessed world. Help me see the riches I already have in You. When I'm tempted to compare and despair, remind me that godliness with contentment is true wealth. Thank You for my enough. Amen.

Your Challenge

Do a "contentment fast" this week: avoid online shopping, unfollow accounts that trigger comparison, and each day name five things you're content with in your life. When you feel the urge to buy or compare, pause and practice gratitude instead. Notice how contentment actually feels better than constant wanting.

Take a Moment

Hold your hands open, palms up, and imagine them full of everything you have – relationships, possessions, opportunities. Now close your hands gently, not grasping tightly but holding with gratitude. Feel the satisfaction of having enough. Your hands aren't empty; they're full of exactly what God knows you need right now.

Week 42: Speaking Life into Others

God's Truth

"Death and life are in the power of the tongue, and those who love it will eat its fruits."–Proverbs 18:21 (ESV)

Devotional Thought

You remember exactly how those cruel words felt – like daggers that still hurt years later. But you also remember that one compliment, that encouraging text, those words that lifted you when you were drowning. Words are powerful weapons that can destroy or tools that can build. Every day, you're choosing which one your tongue will be.

Your words literally have the power of life and death. Not physical death, but the death of dreams, confidence, relationships. That sarcastic comment might be someone's final straw. That gossip session might destroy someone's reputation forever. But flip it around – your encouragement might save someone from giving up. Your kind words might be the only positive thing someone hears today.

Speaking life doesn't mean fake positivity or empty compliments. It means choosing to build up instead of tear down, to encourage instead of criticize, to speak truth wrapped in love. It means using your words to call out the good in others, even when they can't see it themselves.

In a world full of criticism and cruelty, your life-giving words are revolutionary. They cost nothing but can change everything. Every conversation is an opportunity to speak life or death. Choose life.

A Prayer for You

God, help me use my words to speak life into others. When I'm tempted to criticize, gossip, or tear down, remind me of my tongue's power. Fill my mouth with encouragement, truth, and love. Let my words be healing balm in a world full of wounds. Make me generous with life-giving words. Amen.

Your Challenge

Send five specific, genuine encouragements this week – not generic "you're awesome" messages, but detailed observations about someone's character, growth, or impact. Include at least one person you don't usually encourage. Watch how speaking life into others transforms both them and you. Life-giving words create life-giving relationships.

Take a Moment

Touch your tongue to the roof of your mouth and feel its physical presence. This small muscle has incredible power – to heal or hurt, to build or break. Imagine your words as seeds being planted in others' hearts. What will grow from what you're planting? Choose to plant flowers, not thorns.

Week 43: When Temptation Feels Overwhelming

God's Truth

"No temptation has overtaken you that is not common to man. God is faithful, and he will not let you be tempted beyond your ability, but with the temptation he will also provide the way of escape, that you may be able to endure it."–1 Corinthians 10:13 (ESV)

Devotional Thought

That temptation you're fighting feels impossible to resist. Maybe it's that relationship you know isn't good, the lie that seems harmless, the habit you can't break, or the compromise everyone else is making. It whispers that you're missing out, that once won't hurt, that you're strong enough to handle it. The pull feels overwhelming, like gravity you can't fight.

Here's what the enemy doesn't want you to know: this exact temptation has been faced and defeated by others before you. You're not uniquely weak or especially targeted. Every human faces temptation, including Jesus himself. The difference is knowing that God always, always provides an escape route. You're never trapped with no way out.

That escape might be calling a friend before you make that choice. It might be literally leaving the situation. It might be remembering Scripture that combats the lie. The way out is always there, but you have to look for it and take it. God won't force you to escape; He provides the door, but you must walk through.

Victory over temptation isn't about being strong enough. It's about being humble enough to run when you need to, to ask for help, to admit you're vulnerable.

A Prayer for You

God, this temptation feels stronger than me. Show me the way of escape You've promised. Give me courage to take it even when everything in me wants to give in. Help me run to You instead of toward what's tempting me. Thank You for never allowing more than I can handle with Your help. Amen.

Your Challenge

Identify your strongest current temptation and create a specific escape plan: Who will you call? Where will you go? What verse will you remember? Practice this escape route even when you're not tempted, like a fire drill. When temptation strikes, you'll have muscle memory for escape rather than having to figure it out in the moment.

Take a Moment

Clench your fists as tight as you can for ten seconds – feel the tension, the effort, the strain. Now release completely. That relief you feel? That's what it's like to release temptation to God instead of trying to fight it alone. Sometimes victory means opening your hands and letting God fight for you.

Week 44: Your Calling Is Unique

God's Truth

"For we are his workmanship, created in Christ Jesus for good works, which God prepared beforehand, that we should walk in them."-Ephesians 2:10 (ESV)

Devotional Thought

She's called to missions in Africa. Your friend feels called to ministry. Another is clearly meant for medicine. Meanwhile, you're still waiting for that dramatic calling, that burning bush moment, that clear sign from heaven about your purpose. You wonder if maybe you missed God's call, if you're not spiritual enough to hear it, or if maybe you don't have a calling at all.

But God's calling rarely comes through skywriting. More often, it's discovered in the intersection of your gifts, passions, and opportunities. That thing you're naturally good at? That injustice that makes you angry? That need you can't ignore? Those might be clues to your calling. God prepared specific good works for you before you were born – not generic works anyone could do, but works requiring your unique combination of experiences, gifts, and personality.

Your calling might not look like anyone else's. Maybe it's creating beauty that points to God, using business to fund kingdom work, or simply being a light in a dark workplace. Not everyone is called to vocational ministry, but everyone is called to minister where they are.

Stop waiting for your calling to be dramatic and start walking in what's already clear. Your calling is already unfolding in how God made you.

A Prayer for You

God, help me discover the unique calling You've placed on my life. Show me how my gifts, passions, and experiences point to Your purpose for me. Give me patience to let my calling unfold and courage to walk in what You've already revealed. Thank You for preparing specific works for me. Amen.

Your Challenge

This week, pay attention to three things: What makes you come alive? What problems burden your heart? What do others say you're gifted at? Look for patterns and intersections. Your calling often hides in plain sight, disguised as "just who you are." Start walking in these areas and watch your calling become clearer.

Take a Moment

Place your hand over your heart and feel your unique heartbeat – no one else's beats exactly like yours. Just as your heartbeat is unique, so is your calling. God doesn't mass-produce purposes. Feel your individual rhythm and trust that God has an individual calling that only you can fulfill.

Week 45: Freedom Through Forgiveness

God's Truth

"Be kind to one another, tenderhearted, forgiving one another, as God in Christ forgave you."-
Ephesians 4:32 (ESV)

Devotional Thought

They hurt you deeply, maybe even repeatedly. The betrayal, the words, the rejection – it all left scars you still feel. Everyone says to forgive, but they don't understand what was done to you. Forgiveness feels like letting them win, like saying what they did was okay. So you hold onto the hurt, replaying it, letting bitterness grow like a weed choking out joy.

But unforgiveness isn't punishing them; it's poisoning you. They've moved on while you're still chained to that moment. Forgiveness isn't saying what they did was acceptable; it's saying you won't let it control you anymore. It's not about them deserving forgiveness; it's about you deserving freedom. When Paul says forgive as Christ forgave you, remember: you didn't deserve His forgiveness either.

Forgiveness is a process, not always a one-time decision. You might have to forgive the same hurt seventy times seven times as it resurfaces. Each time you choose forgiveness, you break another chain. This doesn't mean reconciling with unsafe people or pretending nothing happened. It means releasing your right to revenge and trusting God with justice.

Freedom comes when you realize forgiveness is for you, not them. It's choosing your healing over your hurt.

A Prayer for You

God, I need Your help to forgive because I can't do it alone. This hurt runs so deep, and bitterness feels easier than forgiveness. Give me strength to release this to You. Help me forgive as You've forgiven me. Free me from these chains I've been carrying. I choose freedom over bitterness. Amen.

Your Challenge

This week, take one step toward forgiving someone who hurt you. You don't have to confront them or even tell them – this is between you and God. Maybe it's praying for them, releasing revenge fantasies, or simply saying "I choose to forgive" out loud. Small steps toward forgiveness lead to complete freedom.

Take a Moment

Hold an ice cube in your hand until it becomes uncomfortable. Feel how the cold spreads, how it hurts, how desperately you want to let go. This is what unforgiveness does to your heart. Now drop the ice cube and feel the relief. That's what forgiveness offers – release from the pain you've been gripping.

Week 46: Standing Firm in Your Faith

God's Truth

"Therefore, my beloved brothers, be steadfast, immovable, always abounding in the work of the Lord, knowing that in the Lord your labor is not in vain."–1 Corinthians 15:58 (ESV)

Devotional Thought

Your teacher mocks Christianity in class. Friends question why you "still believe that stuff." Social media constantly challenges your values. Standing firm in your faith feels like standing alone against a hurricane. You're tired of defending what you believe, exhausted from swimming against the current, wondering if it's worth the constant battle. Maybe it would be easier to just blend in, stay quiet, compromise a little.

But Paul calls you to be steadfast and immovable – not stubborn or judgmental, but unshakeable in your core beliefs. This doesn't mean having an answer for every question or winning every argument. It means knowing what you believe and why, then living it out consistently. Your faith isn't meant to be hidden when it's inconvenient or adjusted to fit in.

Standing firm doesn't always look like grand gestures. Sometimes it's quietly choosing integrity, persistently showing love, consistently living differently. It's being the same person on Saturday night that you are on Sunday morning. When you stand firm, you become a lighthouse – others might mock the light, but secretly they're grateful for it when storms come.

Your labor in standing firm isn't in vain. Every time you choose faith over fitting in, you're impacting eternity.

A Prayer for You

God, give me strength to stand firm when everything pushes against my faith. Help me be unshakeable without being unloving. When I'm tired of standing alone, remind me You're standing with me. Give me wisdom to know when to speak and when to simply live out my faith. Make me steadfast. Amen.

Your Challenge

This week, identify one area where you've been compromising your faith to fit in. Make a concrete decision to stand firm in that area, even if it costs you socially. Remember, standing firm doesn't mean being harsh – be strong in conviction but gentle in approach. Watch how authenticity attracts the right people.

Take a Moment

Stand up and plant your feet firmly, shoulder-width apart. Feel how stable this stance is. Try to gently sway – notice how you naturally return to center. This is how God wants your faith to be: firmly planted, stable, able to weather pushes without toppling. Feel that spiritual stability growing in you.

Week 47: Preparing for What's Ahead

God's Truth

"Therefore do not be anxious about tomorrow, for tomorrow will be anxious for itself. Sufficient for the day is its own trouble."–Matthew 6:34 (ESV)

Devotional Thought

Graduation looming. College decisions. Career paths. Adult responsibilities. The future feels like a massive wave about to crash over you, and you're not sure you're ready to swim. Everyone asks about your plans, but honestly? You're just trying to survive today. The pressure to have it all figured out makes you anxious about tomorrow, next year, the rest of your life.

Jesus says something counterintuitive: don't be anxious about tomorrow. This doesn't mean don't prepare or plan. It means don't let future fears rob today's peace. You can be responsible about tomorrow without being anxious about it. Preparation is wisdom; anxiety is wasted energy. One is productive; the other is paralyzing.

Preparing for what's ahead means doing what you can today while trusting God with what you can't control. Study for the test, apply for the scholarship, develop your skills – but don't carry tomorrow's full weight today. God gives grace for each day as it comes, not in advance. The strength you need for tomorrow will be there tomorrow.

Your future is safe in God's hands. He's already there, preparing the way, working things out. Focus on being faithful today, and tomorrow will unfold as it should.

A Prayer for You

God, the future feels overwhelming and I don't feel ready. Help me prepare wisely without drowning in anxiety. Give me peace about tomorrow while being faithful with today. Show me the next step without demanding to see the whole staircase. I trust You with my unknown future. Thank You for going ahead of me. Amen.

Your Challenge

This week, take one concrete step toward your future without obsessing over the whole journey. Apply for one opportunity, learn one new skill, or have one important conversation. Focus on the next right step rather than the entire path. Action reduces anxiety better than endless worrying. Trust God with the steps you can't yet see.

Take a Moment

Cup your hands together and imagine holding water. You can only hold what fits in this moment – trying to grab more makes you lose what you have. This is how to handle the future: hold what belongs to today, letting tomorrow's concerns flow through. God will refill your hands when tomorrow becomes today.

Week 48: Living with an Eternal Perspective

God's Truth

"So we do not lose heart. Though our outer self is wasting away, our inner self is being renewed day by day. For this light momentary affliction is preparing for us an eternal weight of glory beyond all comparison."–2 Corinthians 4:16-17 (ESV)

Devotional Thought

This test feels like everything. That relationship drama seems earth-shattering. Not making the team feels like the end of the world. In the moment, temporary things feel permanent, and small problems feel enormous. You live like this life is all there is, like your current struggles are the final chapter. But Paul calls our worst troubles "light momentary affliction" compared to eternity.

Living with eternal perspective doesn't mean ignoring present realities. It means seeing them in proper proportion. That embarrassing moment? It won't matter in eternity. That achievement everyone's celebrating? It's nice, but temporary. The kindness you showed to that outsider? That has eternal impact. The faith you're developing through trials? That lasts forever.

When you view life through eternity's lens, priorities shift. Popularity becomes less important than character. Comfort matters less than growth. Temporary pleasure loses appeal compared to lasting joy. You stop living for the approval of people who won't even remember you in five years and start living for the God who will love you for eternity.

This perspective doesn't minimize your current experiences; it maximizes their purpose. Every struggle is preparing eternal glory. Every choice is writing your eternal story. Every moment matters because it's connected to forever.

A Prayer for You

God, help me see my life through eternity's lens. When temporary things feel too important, remind me what lasts forever. Give me perspective to see that my current troubles are producing eternal glory. Help me invest in what matters for eternity, not just for today. Shift my focus from temporary to eternal. Amen.

Your Challenge

This week, before making decisions, ask yourself: "Will this matter in eternity?" Use this filter for how you spend time, what you stress about, and where you invest energy. Make one decision differently based on eternal perspective rather than temporary gain. Notice how this shift changes both your choices and your peace.

Take a Moment

Look at something temporary around you – maybe clothes that will wear out or technology that will be obsolete. Now look at a person near you or think of someone you love. Things are temporary; souls are eternal. Feel the weight of that truth. You're not living for temporary things; you're living for eternal impact.

Week 49: The Gift of Community

God's Truth

"And let us consider how to stir up one another to love and good works, not neglecting to meet together, as is the habit of some, but encouraging one another, and all the more as you see the Day drawing near."–Hebrews 10:24-25 (ESV)

Devotional Thought

You've been hurt by church people. Maybe they were judgmental, hypocritical, or cliquish. So you've decided you can follow Jesus alone, without the messy complications of community. Your faith feels safer as a solo journey, where no one can disappoint you, judge you, or let you down. But isolation might feel safer, yet it's not stronger.

God designed faith to be lived in community. Not perfect community – that doesn't exist – but real community where broken people support each other toward wholeness. You need others to stir up your love when you're growing cold, to encourage you when you're ready to quit, to call out your blind spots with grace.

Yes, community is messy because it's made of messy people. But iron sharpens iron through friction. You grow through the challenge of loving difficult people, forgiving failures, and being loved despite your flaws. The community that frustrates you is often the community that's refining you.

Don't let past hurt rob you of present community. Find your people – imperfect believers who are genuinely seeking God. You weren't meant to do faith alone. Even Jesus had twelve close friends, and one of them betrayed Him. Community is risky but necessary.

A Prayer for You

God, I need authentic community but I'm scared of being hurt again. Help me find genuine believers who will encourage my faith. Give me courage to be vulnerable and wisdom to choose community wisely. Help me contribute to community instead of just consuming it. Show me that together is better than alone. Amen.

Your Challenge

This week, take one step toward deeper community: join a small group, invite someone from youth group to hang out, or have a real conversation after church instead of just attending. Push past surface level with at least one believer. Community doesn't just happen; it's built through intentional investment. Be the community you wish existed.

Take a Moment

Interlace your fingers together and notice how they support each other, creating strength no single finger has alone. Try to break this grip – it's much stronger than individual fingers. This is community: individual believers woven together, creating strength none could have alone. You need others, and others need you.

Week 50: Your Voice Matters

God's Truth

"Let no one despise you for your youth, but set the believers an example in speech, in conduct, in love, in faith, in purity."–1 Timothy 4:12 (ESV)

Devotional Thought

Adults dismiss your opinions because you're "just a teenager." Your ideas get overlooked because of your age. You have things to say – about injustice, faith, change – but no one seems to take you seriously. So you stay quiet, believing your voice doesn't matter yet, that you need to wait until you're older to make a difference.

But God doesn't tell Timothy to wait until he's older to lead. He says don't let anyone despise your youth – instead, be an example now. Your age doesn't disqualify your voice; it uniquely qualifies it. You see things adults have become blind to. You have passion they've lost. You speak to your generation in ways they can't.

Your voice matters because it's yours, not despite your age but because of it. That perspective you have? Someone needs to hear it. That story you've lived? It could change someone's life. That passion burning in you? It might spark movement. Don't wait for permission to use your voice. God already gave it.

History is full of young people who changed the world because they didn't wait to be taken seriously. Mary was a teenager when she said yes to God. David was young when he faced Goliath. Your voice matters now.

A Prayer for You

God, help me believe my voice matters even though I'm young. Give me courage to speak up about things that matter. Help me use my voice for Your glory, not my own. When others dismiss me because of my age, remind me that You value what I have to say. Make my voice count. Amen.

Your Challenge

This week, use your voice for something that matters: share your testimony, speak up about an issue you care about, or encourage someone who needs to hear exactly what you have to say. Don't wait for the perfect moment or perfect words. Your authentic voice is more powerful than perfect silence.

Take a Moment

Hum softly, feeling the vibration in your throat. That's your unique voice resonating – no one else's sounds exactly like yours. God gave you this voice not for later, but for now. Feel the power in your throat, the potential in your words. Your voice is a gift meant to be used, not saved for someday.

Week 51: Finish Strong, Start Fresh

God's Truth

"I have fought the good fight, I have finished the race, I have kept the faith."–2 Timothy 4:7 (ESV)

Devotional Thought

The year is ending, and you're evaluating what happened versus what you hoped would happen. Maybe you started strong but lost momentum. Perhaps you made mistakes you wish you could undo. Or possibly you're just tired, feeling like you're limping toward the finish line rather than sprinting. You wonder if it's even worth trying to finish strong when you've already messed up so much.

Paul didn't say he ran a perfect race or fought without getting wounded. He said he finished and kept the faith. That's what matters – not perfection but perseverance. Finishing strong doesn't mean pretending the year was perfect. It means learning from failures, celebrating growth, and ending with intention rather than just letting things fizzle out.

You still have time to finish this chapter strong. That relationship you've been meaning to repair? That habit you wanted to build? That step of faith you've been postponing? It's not too late. How you finish this season sets the tone for how you'll start the next one.

Starting fresh doesn't mean forgetting everything that happened. It means taking the lessons, leaving the guilt, and moving forward with wisdom. God's mercies are new every morning, and definitely new every year. Finish strong, then start fresh.

A Prayer for You

God, help me finish this season strong despite my mistakes and exhaustion. Give me energy for this final push and wisdom to end well. As I prepare to start fresh, help me bring lessons, not baggage. Thank You for new beginnings and second chances. Help me finish strong and start fresh. Amen.

Your Challenge

Choose one thing to finish strong this week: complete a project you started, have a conversation you've been avoiding, or fulfill a commitment you made. Then identify one thing to leave behind as you start fresh. Finishing strong in one area creates momentum for new beginnings in all areas.

Take a Moment

Take a deep breath in, holding all of this year's experiences – the good, bad, and everything between. Now exhale slowly, releasing what needs to be left behind while keeping the lessons. Feel the freshness of that new breath coming in. This is how you finish strong and start fresh: grateful for what was, ready for what's coming.

Week 52: A New Chapter, A New Beginning

God's Truth

"Therefore, if anyone is in Christ, he is a new creation. The old has passed away; behold, the new has come."–2 Corinthians 5:17 (ESV)

Devotional Thought

Here you are, at the end of this devotional journey but the beginning of something new. You're not the same person who started Week 1. You've grown, struggled, learned, and changed. Some weeks you thrived; others you barely survived. But you made it here, and that's worth celebrating. This ending is really a commencement – a beginning of applying everything you've discovered.

Being a new creation doesn't mean your past disappears or your struggles vanish. It means you're constantly being renewed, constantly becoming more like who God created you to be. Every day offers the possibility of newness – new mercy, new strength, new purpose. You don't have to wait for January 1st to start fresh; with God, every moment is a potential new beginning.

This new chapter you're entering? It's unwritten, full of possibility. You're taking with you 52 weeks of truth, tools, and transformation. You've learned you're loved, valued, and called. You've discovered strength you didn't know you had and grace you didn't know you needed.

The journey continues, but you're not walking it alone or un-prepared. You're equipped, empowered, and accompanied by the God who makes all things new.

A Prayer for You

God, thank You for bringing me through this journey. As I step into this new chapter, go with me. Help me apply what I've learned and continue growing. Make me new every day. Thank You for never giving up on me. I'm excited about what You're writing next in my story. Amen.

Your Challenge

Create a "stones of remembrance" moment: identify the three most important truths you've learned this year and decide how you'll carry them forward. Share your growth with some-one who's been part of your journey. Then pray for another teen girl who needs this same journey. Your ending is some-one else's potential beginning.

Take a Moment

Stand at a doorway or window, looking forward. You're standing at the threshold of your new chapter. Behind you is growth, lessons, and experiences that shaped you. Ahead is possibility, purpose, and promise. Take a step forward, literally or symbolically, into your new beginning. God is already there, preparing the way. Welcome to your new chapter!

Discover More Books

Start each day with purpose, peace, and spiritual renewal.

Whether you're guiding teens in faith or growing closer as a family—this devotional series meets you right where you are.

Collect the Whole Series

Devotional for
Parents and Kids

Devotional for
Teen Girls

Devotional for
Teen Boys

Available at major online bookstores

Each book is a spiritual companion. Together, they form a complete journey—personal, relational, and transformative.

Don't wait—bring home the full devotional set and let every day draw you closer to faith, love, and lasting renewal.